Under the Sun and Over the Moon

PICTURES BY
IAN PENNEY
VERSE BY
KEVIN CROSSLEY-HOLLAND

G. P. PUTNAM'S SONS
NEW YORK

FOR CATHERINE

from Ian

FOR ELEANOR CROSSLEY-HOLLAND

from Kevin

First American edition, 1989.
Text copyright © 1989 by Kevin Crossley-Holland.
Illustrations copyright © 1989 by Ian Penney.
All rights reserved. This book, or parts thereof,
may not be reproduced in any form without permission.
Published in 1989 by G. P. Putnam's Sons,
a division of The Putnam & Grosset Group, New York.
Originally published in Great Britain by Orchard Books, 1989.
Printed in Great Britain by Cambus Litho Ltd.

Library of Congress Cataloging-in-Publication Data
Crossley-Holland, Kevin. Under the Sun and Over the Moon.
Summary: A fanciful introduction to numbers and
how they impose order on the world around us.
[1. Counting — Poetry. 2. English Poetry]
I. Penney, Ian, ill. II. Title.
PR6053.R63A86 1989 821'.914 88-32429
ISBN 0-399-21946-3
1 3 5 7 9 10 8 6 4 2

First impression

Under the sun and over the moon,
Ten secret gardens, a long afternoon.

Will you come through these gardens with me,
And look, and count whatever we see?

We'll take this magic bag to hold
Treasures more precious than silver or gold.

I spy one sundial, one folded wing.
One unicorn. One of everything!

One is one and one's alone.
Who likes being on their own?

When we open this wooden door
We'll find out how one leads to more.

If you can see one, the other's there.
What we're looking for is a pair.

Under the blue and over the green,
Their beaks sharp, their eyes keen,

Two thieving magpies fly zigzag:
Let's pop them into our magic bag.

Here are two threecans—three toucans, I mean!
And snails as juicy as I've ever seen.

Three is the number with a double bend
And a beginning, a middle and an end.

The old world itself is made of three:
The earth, the air and the rocking sea.

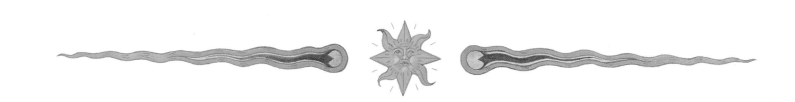

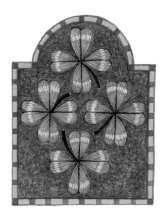

How many geckos? How many bees?
I'm down on all fours: my hands and my knees.

Over the cobbles and under the sun:
I think counting games are fun.

And here, at the foot of this pagoda,
Shall we search for lucky clover?

Five frogs croak, five swallows cry,
Five badgers snuffle. Where am I?

You can count each hoop and each gap,
But a maze like this is a garden-trap.

Look and listen, touch, taste, smell.
Use your senses and use them well.

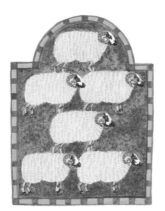

What has six faces and twenty-one eyes?
What has a tongue and never lies?

These silly old sheep cannot tell
The difference between a die and a bell.

Half-a-dozen ewes and rams—
I wonder where they've left their lambs.

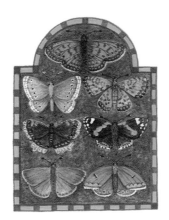

Step into the pointed star
And count each dawn-blue budgerigar.

The days and ages flutter by.
Can you name each butterfly?

Over the moon and under the flag,
Let's catch seven for our magic bag.

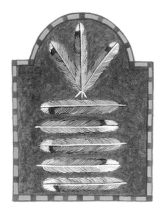

Listen to the fountains playing.
Can you make out what they're saying?

And can you spot the number eight?
Nine and ten will have to wait

While we search this court together
And find each and every feather.

Here are three and three and three
In the garden of harmony.

But cats play tricks with claws like knives.
Cats can smile: they have nine lives.

And how could a girl be so reckless
As to forget her opal necklace?

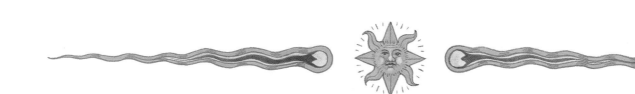

Ten ripe apples from ten ancient trees—
Were apples ever as red as these?

Think of the counting ways we've come:
Over the stars and under the sun

Through secret gardens, gardens of dreams—
The purples and browns, the yellows and greens.

Tumbling out of the magic bag
Come wonders to number and count and add.

Through one door we found all these:
Two joyous magpies,
Three slowcoach snails,
Four four-leafed clover,
Five hopping frogs,
Six bleating sheep,
Seven quivering butterflies,
Eight fluttering feathers,
Nine fireflash opals,
Ten luscious apples.

And there's one object here we did not see.
If *you* can spot it, show it to me.

These are the treasures we did not bring.
We couldn't bag everything!

Ten secret gardens. Our counting is done,
Over the moon and under the sun.

Under the sun and over the moon,
Was it a dream this afternoon?